Take charge of your life

CONTENT

Introduction

"The trouble with the rat race is that, even if you win, you're still a rat" ~ Lily Tomlin ~
There was a time, in the not-so-distant past, when families were expected to give up everything in order to achieve the financial security they craved. Perhaps you remember those decades, perhaps you are too young to recall those times.

Those were the days when climbing the corporate ladder was a revered activity, and wives and children gazed fondly at pictures of the breadwinner in order to remember whether poor, exhausted Dad had blue eyes or brown.

Large companies moved employees from one city to another, like pawns on a chessboard and, if you had any hope of climbing the ladder toward upper management positions, you packed up the wife and kids and moved on from Chicago, to Boston, to New York, to Tokyo.

In the intervening years, the divorce rate climbed, fathers lost touch with their families and died of heart attacks and strokes at an alarming rate. When these men retired, they felt useless and unproductive.

Over the years, the identity of these men had become inextricably tied to their success on the job. New retirees found themselves wondering who they were, and why they were living with women who were complete strangers to them. And, whatever happened to those darling kids who used to live in the house?

Then women entered the workforce in earnest and joined the rat race.

Lest you think that this rat race has come to an end, look to the evidence of stress related death and illness, an increase in the average number of hours worked by employees in the U.S. and around the world, skyrocketing numbers of divorces and children in single-parent families.

And, let us not forget those of us who are responsible for the care of aging parents.

We live in a world of conveniences that were designed to give us more leisure time. But, it would seem that all the informational overload, whirring computers and media blitz has given us is more time for work.

It is not unusual for men and women to work sixty or seventy hours per week on average. Some of us work eighty or ninety hours without batting an eyelash. And, we fool ourselves into thinking we have a life!

3

If you are one of the enlightened few, you have already come to the conclusion that giving up a social and family life is too great a price to pay for career success.
Maybe, you have stress related health problems, perhaps you are not eating right, and you are probably fighting with your spouse, boyfriend or best buddy because you spend too little time with the people you care about most.
You probably can't find the time to return phone calls or send a birthday card to your Aunt Betty.
It doesn't matter if you are a lineman for a utility company, a pizza delivery girl, a corporate executive or an aspiring dancer.
In today's chaotic world, it is a safe bet that you don't have enough time for work, family and friends. And, since your boss holds a tight rein on your paycheck, it is likely that your family and friends are the ones that suffer.

You Are NOT Alone!

"The be-all and end-all of life should not be to get rich, but to enrich the world" ~ B.C. Forbes ~

Did you know that the <u>Society for Human Resource Management</u> has reported that 76% of American workers are considering looking for another job and, further that they estimate there will be 22 million new jobs created over the next ten years, but only 17 million new workers available to fill these jobs?

While every generation of workers has a different set of work expectations, the desire for work/life balance has become one of the foremost goals of every generation in the workforce today.

Baby Boomers are reducing work hours and many 'Thirty-Somethings' are starting their own businesses in order to have more control over their lives and schedules.

A recent study done by the <u>Families and Work Institute</u> illustrates that young workers just starting out in the workforce are choosing to turn down promotional opportunities to achieve greater work/life balance.

Why do you suppose these apple-cheeked, enthusiastic job entrants might take this approach? In a study done with young employees by Families and Workplace, work/life balance was among the top for both genders.

Most of these young adults were raised in families where both parents worked and they experienced the sacrifice and demands placed upon their parents, firsthand.

Not surprisingly, of all the generations in the workforce today, these young adults are the most likely to consider job flexibility and schedules when they look for a job, and it is key to employee retention for companies that employ these young workforce.

The point of all of this background information is to let you know that you are not alone in your desire to find balance.

All generations in all types of jobs are today, looking for balance, less stress, and more time with family and friends. Like you, these people are willing to give it their all when they are at work and they expect to work hard, but in exchange, they want a life.

In essence, YOU ARE NOT ALONE!

If you think that work and family life balance is a small problem, you may be interested to know that, in addition to the few companies that have recognized the issue and taken the lead in establishing life balance programs, there are numerous organizations, foundations, universities and groups doing research on this topic.

Organizations as diverse as religious groups, government agencies, human resource companies and behavioral scientists now study these issues and, not just because it is the right thing to do.

There are real economic advantages to companies that recognize the need for life balance and create a working environment to help their employees live their lives more fully. Companies spend a lot of money training and keeping employees and happy employees will stay longer, live longer and contribute to the company longer.

But, we are just scratching the surface in understanding the true human toll that an unbalanced life takes. Many have studied the evolving societal issues and their roots in overwork and lost community connections.

If you WANT more balance in your life but you wonder whether it is all that important, let's talk about the reasons you NEED this balance.

> *"We are coming to understand health not as the absence of disease, but rather as the process by which individuals maintain their sense of coherence (i.e. sense that life is comprehensible, manageable, and meaningful) and ability to function in the face of changes in themselves and their relationships with their environment" ~ Aaron Antonovsky ~*

Health – Living an unbalanced life where work dominates can significantly affect your health. Long or stressful work hours can cause problems with your heart, your blood pressure, and your sleep cycles.

Studies show a significant increase in heart attack and stroke since the advent of seventy-hour workweeks. Long hours at work and lots of work related travel also encourages poor diet and leaves little time for exercise.

As we become more out of shape, sleep less and experience health problems, we are no longer the powerful asset to our employers, nor can we participate fully in a family and social life.

Emotional Wellness – Your ability to give back to your family, friends and community, and your own emotional stability depends on a balanced life.

As overly dramatic as it sounds, you are likely to experience emotional problems, need counseling and suffer from anxiety attacks or other problems if you have no time to decompress and relax.

There are numerous scientific studies on the benefits of relaxation, recreation and meditation.

6
And these benefits are both physical and emotional.
You can't be ready to take on the issues in your family, support your spouse, parents, siblings and children and your friends if you have no emotional stamina.
If you've spent all of your focus and attention on work and you find yourself so tired at the end of the day that you don't even want to talk to your family, you have a problem. And your family may not wait around for you to resolve it!
The societal impact of 'all work and no play' has damaged and destroyed many a family and the divorce rate continues to climb. Children grow up barely knowing their parents because they are away at work all the time.
Family vacations are a thing of the past in many families. Vacations get postponed and many employees find themselves losing their accrued vacation time because they have 'rolled it over' for so many years and just NOT taken the vacation they deserved.
Your emotional reserves are depleted. You have no patience with yourself or others. You are short on sleep and even on time to think about what you want for dinner.
Is it any wonder that psychologists and psychiatrists are busier than ever?
Stress - We have talked about the health implications related to 'all work and no play' but stress is its own health factor.
Even if you like your job, if you have no time for anything else, stress will get you eventually.
We'll talk more about stress later and you'll get some tips on how to eliminate or mitigate stress so that your body and mind will be better able to handle whatever comes your way.
For now, what you need to understand is that stress can affect your physical and emotional health and that, over time, it can make you very sick. If you are not in a position to change jobs or otherwise make a major change to relieve stress, learn how to handle it better.
We're not talking about taking five years of classes here. We are talking about simple techniques you can use to help balance your life.
Remember that work/life balance is not just a question of the hours you spend in one place or another. It is also a question of how balanced you feel and how you react to things.
No matter how much time you have with your family and friends, you will enjoy it more if you are able to balance YOURSELF.

If you can become less of a victim of stress and overwork and take control of your own reaction to stress, you will live longer and be happier at work and at home.

Family and Community – Government and university studies support the idea that the 'all work and no play' lifestyle contributes to divorce, dysfunction in the family, and lack of involvement and investment in the community and neighborhood.

As the community grows apart and neighbors become strangers, emotional and family support for things like childcare, help with aging parents and support following trauma and tragedy become real issues.

The community turns to the government to supply services to fill this gap, taxes rise and people remain strangers.

Families struggle with alternating schedules, and children fail to thrive emotionally and physically.

Divorce is rampant and single parents are under even more stress with even less time to pay attention to children. So, things deteriorate even more!

Role models for marriage, relationships and juggling time and family are important to a child's adult relationships. If we do not provide those positive role models, we perpetuate the problem.

It is interesting to note that the generation of children now in the work force has started to rebel against jobs and employers that require ridiculous hours and dedication beyond the call of duty.

They understand the toll this type of career takes on a life. They grew up in families that suffered this impact.

Perhaps our greatest hope for change lies in this generation of seasoned veterans of dysfunctional families.

Productivity – If your employer believes that your eighty-hour workweek is giving him more benefit, he should look at the statistics and information gathered by human resource companies and companies that focus on efficiency and productivity.

It is a fact that the human brain needs downtime and rest and recreation to recycle. Think about your own life and the times when you had to work long hours to get something finished.

Perhaps you found that you could barely focus after a certain number of hours. There is a reason that coaches that teach good study habits tell students not to cram for eighteen hours before an exam, but rather to spread out the studying and mix in recreation.

Take a walk; talk with friends to regain your clarity and focus.

If you and your employer truly want to take the best advantage of your time, you need to take time for yourself.

You will spend less time reworking things you've done wrong, mistakes you've made and details you've missed. And your employer will get better quality and output regardless of your job.

Pilots are subject to time constraints and can only spend so many hours in the air because airlines learned a long time ago that a tired and overworked pilot could make critical errors.

In lengthy neurosurgery or heart surgery, surgeons take breaks and leave the operating room to clear their heads and rest.

Again, these habits and techniques were learned the hard way and only when critical mistakes were made did these work policies change. You wouldn't want a tired doctor working on your open heart, would you?

Life Goals – Everyone has goals. And you are probably no exceptions. You may have work and career-related goals like promotions, expanded responsibilities, and recognition as an expert in your industry.

These are all fine, but be sure you don't just focus on your job. Many people come to identify their success in life by their position in their job and the recognition they get there.

If they become disabled or sick, or if they retire, they suddenly find that they don't know themselves anymore.

They have no identity at work so they don't know who they are. They may have lost family and friends or have become strangers to these people, unaware of the important events that happened at home while they were at work.

So, they have to get to know themselves and their loved ones all over again. For some, this is an impossible task.

Be sure you set personal goals, family goals and general goals in your life for growth and happiness.

Whether it is going on for a Masters Degree in the fine art you love, learning how to fly a plane, or playing the piano, you should have goals that keep you involved in other parts of your life.

While you are setting goals, don't forget your family goals. Perhaps you have always wanted to take your wife to Hawaii. Set the goal and a timetable and do it!

Remember that life goals can include giving back to the community and to others. It is interesting to note that, since so many people cannot achieve their personal goals because of career obligations, we now find it difficult to get baseball coaches to volunteer their time, or to get people to volunteer in hospitals and work for the community as a volunteer ambulance driver or firefighter.

It's Time to Take Action

"This strange disease of modern life, With its sick hurry, its divided aims" ~ Matthew Arnold ~

Now that we've discussed the reasons work/life balance is important, and you know that others feel as you do, what do you do about the problem?

You may hate what has happened to your life. But, you probably don't know how to change the landscape. You will be happy to know that you CAN change your life.

Whether you make this decision for health reasons, relationship reasons or simply out of the need to get control over your own life, you have more than enough justification and motivation to make the move.

However, you need to make a firm commitment to this change. Be realistic about how fast and how far you can go with this plan.

But, let's be clear about something! What we are talking about here is not quitting your job and hoping that someone will donate money to the cause.

There is a real difference between achieving balance in your work and family life and the idea that you don't have to work at all.

Work is part of life, and it is healthy and constructive. It pays the bills; it gives us the reward of real accomplishment and feeling of useful participation in the community and in society.

What we are talking about here is the rational balance of your work and social life – a balance that is all too rare in today's society, and one whose absence has caused sky-high healthcare costs and a dramatic increase in stress, psychological and relationship problems.

Now that we are clear on the goals and reasons for work/life balance, let's continue!

If you've decided to jump off the merry-go-round and seek some occasional solace with your family and friends, you must have a plan for your escape.

First, and foremost, you must set goals! Involve your boss, co-workers, friends and family in the process and keep the lines of communication open, and you'll end up where you want to be.

Sounds easy, doesn't it?

Depending on your age and how long you have run the rat race, you may find it harder than you thought it would be but with perseverance and the right support network, you can succeed.

11
Are you ready? Good!
Then, without further ado, let's proceed!

'The Career' Versus 'The Job'

"Work expands so as to fill the time available for its completion" ~ C. Northcote Parkinson ~

Before you decide to tell your boss that you simply must have more time off to spend with the family, you'll need to consider a few things.

First, most large companies now support balanced life plans – in other words, they recognize the need for their employees to take vacations, take time off to go to the doctor with a sick child, and get home for dinner at a reasonable hour.

But, in some companies, that commitment is lip service only. In other words, what the human resource policies say is one thing. The reality is quite something else.

In smaller companies, all bets are off!

Some companies are so small that they are not subject to government regulations regarding hours but it is important for you to understand that in today's world, no company in the U.S. can abuse an employee by working them 24 hours a day.

Remember, there are labor laws to protect you.

The first thing you need to do is to understand your rights. If you live in a country other than the U.S., you will have to look at the labor laws there to determine what you can expect when you go to talk to your boss.

Remember, the better prepared you are, the better chance you will have at getting what you need. If your boss does not know the law, you'll need to be prepared to educate her.

Before you begin to execute your plan to balance your life, you'll want to think carefully about your job, and your career goals.

You'll find some thought-provoking considerations below.

Think carefully about each of these things, and add your own considerations to the list, if you have some that are specific to your own job.

If you really want balance and change in your life, you have to plan for it and then carefully execute the plan with dedication and persistence.

Here are some things to consider:

🕐 Are you a member of a union? If so, there are rules regarding your work hours and these must be enforced. You can talk to a union steward to get help with this.

🕐 Do you have a contract that requires you to work certain hours? If you do, you may have to change jobs to get the balance you want in your life.

🕐 If you are in a position that is critical to the company – in other words, no one else can do what you do – then you may out of luck when it comes to getting reduced hours.

🕐 Are you making a ridiculous amount of money in your job? If you are, your hours are probably not negotiable.

The company you work for certainly expects you to earn the money they pay you and the generous compensation is meant to reward you for the hours and stress. Again, you may have to change jobs and, at the same time, change your salary expectation.

🕐 Does everyone in your company and/or department work crazy hours? There are some jobs - like technical support in a company with critical data stored on servers, or networks – where you will not have the option to negotiate your departure time on certain days.

Perhaps, on other days when things are quiet and slow, you can ask your boss to let you leave early and/or get compensatory time to reward you for the crazy hours you are expected to work during an emergency.

Don't despair if you are a trauma nurse, or you work in the operating room or in other jobs where you have to work really tough shifts.

Many hospitals, fire departments and other such companies are now using a 4-day on, 3-day off schedule or other schedules that let these critical workers spend more time with their families.

These flexible schedules also allow employees to schedule daytime appointments, and to decompress from the sometimes-stressful experiences and events that occur while they are on the job.

If your employer does not participate in these schedules, perhaps you want to take your skills elsewhere.

Seasonal jobs may give you the opportunity to negotiate hours, as well. Put your nose to the grindstone during Christmas hours in a retail store, or summer hours in a surf shop, and ask for extra time off to reward your dedication during the off-season.

- Look carefully at your position and determine if you have a 'job' or a 'career'. If you are in it for the long haul and hope to continue the climb to upper management, you can expect to work much longer hours and endure a lot more stress.

  Can you take another job in a lower stress environment, perhaps a company that prides itself on being 'family friendly' and still get into management?

  If you want to stay in the company you are in, and continue to climb, and if your company is not dedicated to a balanced life for their employees, you may find it very difficult, if not impossible, to balance your life.

- If you are in a position to do so, and your company does not recognize the need for and value of a balanced work and family approach, consider going to your human resource department or to your manager and starting a grass roots movement to look at this issue.

  Of course, management may immediately think you simply want to do less work than they want you to accomplish. To counter this, you'll need to arm yourself with information.

  There are all kinds of studies on increased productivity, employee retention and performance that support the decision to create a balanced work and family environment.

  Companies like DuPont, Motorola, Hewlett-Packard, Marriott International, Eddie Bauer Inc. and many others have instituted these programs and your employer may look to these leaders to get some ideas.

  There are resources available online for you and for your company. These resources include seminars for company employees, and documents that teach managers and employees how to better manage time and workload so that the employee can accomplish more work, and produce excellent output – all in less time.

  Look at sites like these:

  > http://www.bc.edu/centers/cwf/
  > http://cwfr.la.psu.edu/research.htm
  > http://www.familiesandwork.org/
  > http://www.workandfamily.org/
  > http://www.workfamily.com/
  > http://hrweb.mit.edu/worklife/index.html

http://www.uml.edu/centers/CFWC/

You'll notice that many of these sites are sponsored by universities and these universities often participate with companies to help them execute a work/life balance strategy.

In exchange, the university gains valuable insight and knowledge that they use to advance their studies.

You will also notice that many of these sites have online courses, or self-paced courses to walk management and/or employees through the process of planning for and executing a balanced work/life program.

- If the reason you are working really long hours, under tremendous stress is that your boss is a lunatic, then you need to change jobs. Before you do that, you have to honest with yourself.

Be sure that you aren't contributing to the problem and that you have honestly tried to improve your relationship. Be sure that you don't make things worse by offering to work longer hours or take someone else's shift because you feel guilty. If your attitude and feelings of obligation about work are contributing to your long hours and burying you work you can never finish, you have to make some changes in your work habits. This may sound easy, but it isn't necessarily so. Many people function from guilt and take on more than they should because they want their bosses and co-workers to like them or they think they will get a promotion or raise, when they actually aren't required to do more than perform well in order to be recognized.

If you have emotional issues about what is enough, or how to be well liked on the job, you have to address those.

Some companies offer job coaches, or life coaches to help you through these obstacles. If not, consider getting a life coach on your own time or go to a counselor and work through your issues.

Remember, it is important to do a good job and even, many times, to go the extra mile, but you should never put yourself in a position where you do all the work while other people get paid the same amount or more and get promotions or time off when you do not.

If you get to this point in your reading and you have become convinced that you would have to change companies and jobs in order to achieve the balance you desire, don't be discouraged.

While you may think there are no companies out there that stress work/life balance, you would be surprised at the number of companies – small and large – that are embracing this philosophy as a way to attract and retain good employees.

Companies as diverse as Chubb, J.C. Penney, PrintingForLess, and RSM McLadrey have programs in place, and report that their employees and managers have enthusiastically embraced the work/life balance.

Employees are working together in teams, better than ever before, to ensure that the work flow continues when they are away at attending a daughter or son's kindergarten graduation or taking advantage of a four day work week to catch up on their golf game.

As this trend continues, and more companies are forced to consider this balanced environment to attract and keep valuable employees and skills, your search for the perfect company will become much easier.

In the meantime, look around.

These companies are much easier to find than they used to be and it is more acceptable today to say that you want this balance – whether you are male or female, young or experienced, or working as an executive or a retail clerk.

The last area we need to discuss in the work half of the work/life balance is Time Management.

This may not apply to everyone, but it certainly applies to many people.

In surveys done across many job categories, including construction, service industries like hotels and restaurants, small business owners and corporate moguls, a large percentage of those surveyed said that they felt they needed to improve their time management skills so that they didn't need to spend as much time at work.

Many wanted to reduce the time they had to spend reworking tasks they had already performed because they had done it wrong the first time.

You will find a few simple tips below, to get your time under control.

If you do these things, you will find that, even in the most stressful and time-consuming jobs, you can reduce the hours you spend at work, and arrive home in a less stressed, more family-friendly frame of mind!

Make a 'To Do' List – Then put these items in order, starting with the most critical. If you could only get one thing done today, what would be the most important?

Cross the items off the list as you complete them, and don't be distracted. Stay focused!

Since we all have interruptions, be sure that, if you don't accomplish the items toward the bottom of you list on that day, you add them to your list the next day so you don't drop them.

Use a daily planner if that makes things easier.

Don't Waste Time – Use your spare minutes well. Take the train to work instead of driving and use that time to read critical reports you may have to review, or read your new equipment training manual on the bus on the way home.

If you are going to take a break during the day and there is someone you have to see, stop by their office and grab them to go for coffee, then talk about the issue and resolve it while you are walking out in the sunshine and enjoying your java.

You'll feel like you took a break AND got something accomplished at the same time.

Just Say 'No' - If your boss wants you to work late and you have a family engagement, but you could work late the next night or come early in the morning, suggest alternatives and see if those will work.

Don't be so quick to accept the command without probing to find out if there is another way to handle it.

If a co-worker asks you to lunch and you MUST finish a report by 3:00, politely decline the invitation and suggest dinner or coffee later instead, and get the report done.

That way you don't have to give up the pleasurable experience, but you won't be stressed out and working until 9:00 p.m. with your boss standing over your shoulder bemoaning the delay.

If the project your boss dumps on your desk is a 'rush' but she already gave you something that must be completed today, ask for clarification on priorities and give your boss a reasonable projection of how long it will take to do both projects and whether you can do both.

Don't just take the project on and then not finish the other task she gave you, or you will both be unhappy. Speak up!

Know Your Brain – Do you know what the Circadian Clock is? It's that little clock in your brain that controls when you feel the most wide awake and when you want to go to sleep.

If you are a morning person, attack the most difficult problems in the morning when your brain is the sharpest. That way you won't have to rework the problem the next day when you discover that the 'afternoon you' made the wrong decision about the budget.

Get Enough Sleep – Your brain can operate on a short nap for a day, but if you are not sleeping enough, you will not think well or process information and you'll make mistakes and end up staying late to fix them.

Advertise Your Schedule - If you hate getting phone calls first thing in the morning, before you get your day organized and have your first cup of coffee, then let your calls go to voicemail until you feel ready to take the calls.

You will be more focused and get more accomplished, instead of having to say, "I'll have to get back to you on that" after hearing a ten minute explanation of the latest crisis.

Be Your Own Master – Sit down with a pencil and paper or a calendar and figure out how much free time you have.

Schedule and plan your activities at work and get your personal and family obligations on the calendar. Treat these personal obligations with the same respect you would treat a business meeting.

Don't cancel personal appointments unless it is a real work emergency and, in the case where you MUST cancel, reschedule immediately and apologize to your friend or family member.

Explain what is happening so they don't think they are unimportant to you. And be sure to keep the appointment you make with them the next time!

Don't Procrastinate or Agonize – Don't spend time during a family dinner worrying about the presentation tomorrow. Put your mind back where it belongs. Worrying never helped anyone accomplish a goal.

If you are prepared for the presentation, just do it. If you aren't prepared, it is doubtful that you will be prepared by the morning.

So don't worry about it.

Don't procrastinate because you don't like a particular activity.

FIRST do those things you dislike the most, and then reward yourself by doing the things you most like to do.

Put things on the calendar and stick to the dates – don't talk yourself into waiting or you will just have more to do tomorrow!

19

Train and Delegate – Don't tell yourself you don't have the time to show someone else how to do that job that you REALLY don't have to do.

Take the time to teach them and soon you will have a well-oiled team machine going, with everyone doing what they are capable of doing.

Don't worry that the employee will take your job.

If you create a functioning team with everyone performing well, your reputation as a manager, mentor and coach will give you a shot at that promotion you want.

And, when you don't have to do ALL the work yourself, you will find a lot more time to get those other tasks done and still get out of the office, shop or store on time and get home for Mom's birthday dinner.

The other benefit to this time management technique is that, when you go on vacation or take that long-awaited three day weekend to go skiing, you will not have to call the office every hour to be sure there isn't some problem you have to solve.

Your family will greatly appreciate having your attention on a dedicated basis for a few days of much-needed bonding.

And don't overlook job-sharing programs, and cross-training as concepts that will nicely cover responsibilities and ensure that the company keeps running when you are not there.

Get Organized – It is impossible to manage your schedule if you can't find things or if you have to recreate work or reinvent something because you lost it.

Take that Action List to heart and, starting today, put a task at the top of the list to organize files, or to rearrange the store or inventory so it is easier to stock or to find things.

Once you have things organized, don't let them get out of control again.

The only way to justify the work involved in that reorganization is if you KNOW you will never have to go through it again!

Keep a Realistic Perspective - Setting unrealistic goals is a mistake – whether it is the completion date of a software project, or the time you think you can deliver that report to your manager, if you underestimate the time required to get the work done, you will end up working late and you'll look bad to your boss.

Be realistic about when you plan to complete tasks and do your homework to be sure that you can accomplish the task in this timeframe.

Consider other ways to get the job done if you think these considerations will help you meet the deadline faster, but don't promise what you can't deliver.

It is good to set goals that challenge you, but if you can never reach the goal, you will not do yourself any favors.

We'll talk about your goals and what you really want in a little while, but for right now, you need to think realistically about your dedication to a balanced life.
It will come with some sacrifices in certain areas, but it will reap many benefits in your life – health, relationships and happiness to name a few.
Is balancing your work and your family life important enough for you to make some tough choices? If it isn't, you may not get the balance you want.
Decide NOW! Start TODAY!

Keeping the Home Fire Burning

"Work is the meat of life, pleasure the dessert" ~ Bertie Charles Forbes ~

We've talked about the work environment and some of the considerations there. Now, it's time to open the Pandora's Box and talk about your family situation.

Unless you are starting your career fresh, with no history, you probably have a lot of fence mending to do.

Your family and friends may be very discouraged and disappointed that you haven't found a way to balance your life and spend more time with them.

If this is the case, you need to talk to your family and your friends and tell them what you have in mind. Tell them that you are going to dedicate yourself to achieving balance in your life and ask them for their opinion.

Remember, that you don't have to take every suggestion anyone gives you, and make clear that you will do what you feel is best in the end, but you want his or her thoughts on the topic.

Listen carefully and be honest with yourself and with your friends and family about what you can expect to achieve.

Don't promise what you can't deliver.

If there are going to be issues on which you must compromise, if you will have to look for another job where you will make less money in order to achieve your goals, be sure they understand that sacrifice, as well.

There should be no surprises. Before you start this discussion, put some thoughts of your own on paper and think through what you can achieve, realistically.

Be prepared to talk to your family and friends and have some idea of how you will execute your plan.

You can change this plan and work with your family to adjust it, but you need to go in with SOME plan or you will face a chaotic mix of accusation, opinion and emotion.

Here are some links to get you started. After you look at these links, you may have other questions and ideas. Keep track of these.

Write them down so that you can address all the issues with your boss and your family.

The Center for Work and the Family

http://www.centerforworkandfamily.com/
National Institute of Health
http://wflc.od.nih.gov/
Questia Online Library for Work and Family
http://www.questia.com/library/sociology-and-anthropology/relationships-and-the-family/family/work-and-family.jsp?CRID=work_and_family&OFFID=sel&KEY=work_family&LID=14582939
PBS
http://www.pbs.org/workfamily/
Bella Online
http://www.bellaonline.com/site/workandfamily

If you do your homework online, you'll find many more links that are useful.

There are sites that target working womens' issues, sites that specifically target stress at work and many other topic-specific sites to help you deal with your job and your family in a way that makes life easier for the ones you love.

When you come up some ideas to discuss with your family, be sure you preface your discussion by explaining that you want to change your focus and balance.

Tell them that you know that work has been pulling you away and you want to fix that. Just knowing that you recognize the problem and want to work on it, will make them feel better.

If you have children, talk to your spouse or significant other before you call a family meeting.

Consider how you want to address this with the kids and remember that children will often take what you say very literally so don't play fast and loose with your language. Think carefully about what you want to say and the words you will use and only promise them what you can deliver.

Don't lead them to think you are quitting your job to stay home with them and play all day – unless you've just won the lottery, of course!

It is likely that whatever plan you have to regain some balance in your life will take awhile to execute, so don't promise that everything will be fixed by tomorrow.

You may have to look for, find and train in a new job.

You may have to cut back on expensive purchases and lifestyle.

Be sure everyone is on board before you pull away from the dock! Make sure the children understand how important this to them and to you and what they will get in return.

You may think that is clear, but depending upon their age, it may not be as clear to them as it is to you and your spouse.

As you make your plans for work/life balance, consider these things:

You may be trading long hours for financial stress, if you are going to take a job for less pay. How will that impact the family and your commitment to this process? Can you find ways to offset some of the impact of this financial decision?

If you are not changing jobs, but you are going to manage your schedule in a different way, how will you change your family schedule to accommodate that?

Can you eat dinner a bit later, so you can eat together as a family? Can you take the children to an early movie to spend time with them before you take that afternoon shift? If you and your spouse work different shifts to be home with the children, include time in your plan for the two of you to get together. If you have to make a date to do that, don't be shy about it.

Can you share a cup of coffee in between shifts? Get up a little earlier? Go to bed a little later? Don't neglect that most important person in your life.

Whatever your schedule is, find some quiet time for yourself, and quiet time with your family without the TV playing in the background. Eat dinner together or play a game. When you go grocery shopping with the children, take a break and go to the back of the store for a cup of coffee and a doughnut. The kids will appreciate the time with you and it will make the shopping more tolerable. Find time to do something as a family at least once a week. Order a pizza so you don't have to cook and spend the time playing a board game, or taking a hike.

Pick an activity that everyone likes and just do it! It sounds corny, but even a few minutes of this kind of activity will give you a lot more balance in your life.

Assuming you have done what you need to do to find more time away from work, or to change jobs, you may think you've now completed the transition. But, that is far from the truth.

The fact is that balancing work and family – in short balancing your life – can be a constant challenge.

There are lots of distractions and, that extra time you've carved out of your work schedule will not do your friends and family much good if you spend it parked in front of the TV or computer, instead of with the ones you love.

To complete your plan, you'll need to develop two traits: *Self-discipline and awareness.* Most of us suffer from the absence of both of these traits, but if you focus on them and on breaking bad habits that distract you and take you away from what you really want to do, you will be much happier.

First, let's talk about self-discipline. The absence of this trait is what gets you off track. It is what pulls you to the computer casino game instead of out to the back yard to play a game of catch with your son.

It is what makes you put off those chores and tasks – whether they are home or work related – that then spring full-grown at 8:00 p.m. to remind you that you must complete them before morning.

And you spend another evening in the den or office crunching numbers for bills, or finishing that project you put off, instead of tucking your daughter into bed or visiting with your husband over a glass of wine.

When you catch yourself listening to the news anchor while your wife tries, in vain, to tell you about her day, reach for the remote and turn off the TV.

Self-discipline and breaking old habits go hand in hand. If you've gotten used to becoming a vegetable when you get home from work, it won't matter how much extra time you get with your family.

You will simply fritter it away!

Awareness is also important. Become aware of what you are doing, what you are saying and every time you catch yourself taking things for granted, remember that the little time you have with your family and friends is important and pay attention.

Listen to what your friend, spouse or child is saying to you.

Listen to your father when he calls you on the phone and wants to tell you about the fish he caught. And look for the opportunities to grab a special moment during the chaos of your week. Don't just slide through life.

Make it happen!

There are two other things you may want to consider in your quest for balance at home. These two things will give you more balance and engender better relationships.

And once you've laid the groundwork, they will pretty much manage themselves.

The first consideration is: Rules!

Perhaps you are thinking that you hate rules. Most people do, but they are a necessary evil in life.

Think about it! Laws are nothing more than societal rules that keep the wheels greased and running and prevent chaos.

Rules in your work/life balance will give you and your family structure and, if and when the rules are bent or broken, the exceptions must be carefully explained.

Your family and you must know that you mean business and, only when there are extenuating circumstances, are the rules bent or broken.

But, Rules are never ignored!

Rules apply to when and how the family will get together and to things like whether your child can stay out late on a school night or whether they are expected to attend a family birthday party.

They also apply to YOU as they relate to when you'll come home from work and whether you will attend the Friday night movie with the family or beg off and say you have to work. How often will you make it to the league soccer game or the lacrosse games?

Rules are for everyone.

A good way to establish these rules is to have the family sit down together and develop the list. Everyone can vote and everyone's opinion counts. Some rules may be very simple and some may be temporary.

But if you have a set of rules printed or typed on your refrigerator, you and your family will feel more confident in your balance and will know better what to expect in a certain situation.

But, don't expect the family to obey the rules, if you don't obey them. You have to keep your end of the bargain too!

The second consideration is: Communication!

To keep your life and the life of your family in balance, you need time and attention. But you also need communication.

Even if your job is demanding, you can balance your life better with your family if you make them part of the equation.

Your job and what you do when you are away from home on business should not be a mystery.

If you have to go out of town, tell the family where you are going, when you will be back and why you are going and use telephone, email and text messaging to keep in touch so they don't feel like you are on another planet.

If you say you are going to call at a certain time, be sure to do so!

Don't leave them hanging. Leave silly notes or messages to find while you are away and bring home little gifts.

You don't have to bring anything expensive – some kids get a kick out of the small ketchup bottles that come with your room service order.

That is easy, and inexpensive and it lets them know you are thinking about them.

If you can have dinner together at night, do so and keep the conversation pleasant. Don't choose dinnertime to bring up bad grades or that boyfriend you can't stand.

Your kids will not want to have dinner with you, if you do that.

Make the mealtime conversation pleasant, and keep the distractions out of the dining room. No TV, music or other disruptions.

Family meetings are a great way to keep the lines of communication open and, again, everyone's opinion counts and everyone gets the floor to say what they need to say.

Keep the meetings constructive and informative and talk about whatever is going on in your lives.

A twenty-minute family meeting will give you a chance to touch base and feel connected and, even if you are working long hours, you will not feel like a stranger in your own home.

Agree on how and when you will communicate throughout the day – even when you are not home. Is your child expected to call you and check in when he gets home from football practice?

27

Create a mail slot or an 'in box' for all the notices from school, permission slips and other items. A mailbox for each person in the family is even better, if you have the room. Then, you can leave little notes for each other to keep in touch, or just to say hello, or 'I love you'.

How is Your Social Life?

"Life is painting a picture, not doing a sum" ~ Oliver Wendell Holmes ~

While we are on the subject of your personal life, let's not forget your friends. Everyone has them and everyone needs them.

Friends are a necessary social extension and they provide an outlet, a group of like-minded people who share values, though perhaps not always every opinion.

Time out with friends, whether they are old high school buddies or friends you've made at work, is important.

A movie, a cup of coffee, an occasional dinner, perhaps even sharing an activity you both like, such as bowling, golf, baseball, slot machines, a book club, or going to the movies, the theater or the ballet.

All of the techniques we discussed for your family life can also be applied to your friends.

Above all, keep in touch. Schedule events and get-togethers with a realistic eye to what you can achieve.

Many people work long hours, have demanding jobs and still manage to participate in monthly groups, or scheduled activities. And, this is a welcome relief from their grueling work schedule.

Put the appointments on your calendar just as you would any business meeting, and be dutiful about keeping the appointment even if it seems a guilty pleasure during that critical crunch season at work.

If you must cancel, communicate clearly with your friend(s) and let them know why you have to reschedule.

DO reschedule.

Don't leave it to chance or you will never get together.

When you go out with friends, even if they are co-workers, use your newly learned skills in self-discipline to keep you out of the realm of work discussion.

Don't talk shop, or you will not get away from the stress you tried to leave behind at the office. It is a hard habit to break, and it may take some time and focus to learn the new habit.

You can make it fun by agreeing that the person who breaks the 'don't talk shop' code first will have to buy a round of drinks or coffee, or has to pay for dinner.

You'd be amazed at how quickly your co-workers will learn the lesson!

If you have a friend, or a group of old college chums with whom you love to socialize, try to pick a monthly or weekly date – the second Tuesday of every month, for example – and get together then.

Everyone will look forward to these occasions and you won't feel so deprived of social contact.

During times of high stress and long hours, take the time to go out for a walk or get a cup of coffee or have lunch with someone outside the office.

Get away from the people you see in the halls every day and get a breath of fresh air.

You'll feel much better.

Don't give up the activities and friends you love. Exercise and socialization are key to balancing your life and even though you may feel they can be postponed until a time when your career is not on high speed, your health will benefit from the short breaks and scheduled visits you insist on taking.

We'll talk more about stress and exercise later, and how these figure into life balance. Right now, let's focus on your friends.

If your friends have fallen by the wayside with the advent of your most recent and most hectic job, you need to get some more friends fast.

Man does not live by work alone!

And though your family is very important to you, your friends serve a different purpose. They are often more honest with you than your family can be and they will forgive and forget without the same intimate emotional attachment of a spouse, a mother or a brother. You can count on them to make you laugh and to share your successes and failures. They are part of your psychological armor and a necessary part of your life's balance.

If you need to reconnect with friendship, you can often find someone with whom you share common values at work, or in an industry association or club.

Or you may find a friend that shares a passion for a sport or an activity while attending a sporting event or on line at the movie theater.

Seek out friends actively and don't be afraid to invite your new friend for a drink or coffee. There is no harm done if the friendship does not blossom.

Friends make you more interesting and expand your horizons.

And, they keep you from becoming a boring, 'all work and no play' kind of person.

Again, you have to be disciplined, have a plan and pay attention, to take advantage of these opportunities.

> *"Work is the greatest thing in the world, so we should always save some of it for tomorrow"*
>
> *~ Don Herold ~*

Setting Expectations

Up until now, we have only touched on expectations, but they are perhaps the most important part of your balancing plan. Expectations come into play in several ways.

First, there are YOUR expectations.

What is it that you expect to get from a more balanced life? More free time? A closer relationship with your spouse? The time to pursue an advanced degree?

Maybe, you want to learn to ride a horse? Any or all of these things are fine goals, but your expectation to achieve balance must take into consideration that some of these goals will take MORE time away from your family.

So, the first thing you have to do is to get it straight in your own mind. What is 'balance' for you?

Is it more time for yourself? More time for your family? Don't make a promise to get more work/life balance and then squander that balance with poor planning.

What do you expect to achieve? How will this balance change your life?

Are you expectations realistic for the planned timeframe and actions you want to take or are you dreams too large?

Once you have your own expectations under control, you'll need to look to your employer and your family and friends to be sure that you understand and can meet their expectations.

It is all well and good that you expect to regain some balance in your life but if your employer still thinks you should work eighty hours per week, you aren't likely to get far.

Put it on paper. Then talk to the people most important to you and those whose support is crucial – like your boss – to find out what THEY expect. Then compare notes and figure out if everything is aligned.

If it isn't, you'll have to adjust the plan. Once you get the plan right, you can move forward more quickly and with more success.

Setting Goals

"Time is the coin of your life. It is the only coin you have, and only you can determine how it will be spent. Be careful lest you let other people spend it for you" ~ Carl Sandburg ~

Now, let's talk about Goals. Like any other important life decision, you have to have goals or you are shooting in the dark.

To set Goals for your work/life balance, you have to take your expectations and translate them into the 'what' of what you want to achieve and the 'when'. Be as specific as possible.

For example, if you are going to look for a new, less demanding job, your goals might include the industry you want to work in, the type of job you want to get and how much money you want to make, as well as when you want to get the job.

Here are some examples to get you started:

"My goal is to get a job with one of the Top Ten banks in the U.S., as a Bank Manager, by May of 2006"

"Reduce the number of hours I work by 10 hours per week in time for John's 2006 Little League Season"

"Visit my mother every Sunday for at least three hours"

"Train 2-3 people on my staff to take over the bookkeeping process by January of next year"

"Schedule and keep a weekly date with Mary for dinner and a movie"

Simple, right?

Remember, the best way to set goals is to word them simply but specifically!

That way you can measure your success without trying to guess whether you succeeded.

The next task at hand is to figure out HOW to achieve your goals.

Remember that your expectations and goals must be realistic or you will never get to where you want to be!

Now it is time to figure out just how realistic your expectations and goals are, because you have to establish a plan to achieve those goals!
Let's take the first example and see what we can do with that one.
> "My goal is to get a job with one of the Top Ten banks in the U.S., as a Bank Manager, by May of 2006"

To establish a workable plan for this goal you would need to consider the following questions.

- What are the top 10 banks in the U.S.?
- How do you find out what jobs are available at each bank?
- Are you qualified for the Bank Manager jobs in these banks?
- Will these job openings require you to move your family to another location?
- Are there job placement agencies you can use to find these jobs and arrange for interviews?
- Do you have an up-to-date resume?
- Do you have the appropriate wardrobe for this job?
- Do you have good references?
- Do your family and/or spouse support this decision?
- Is it realistic to expect that you can research, find and get this job by May, 2006?

You can probably think of more questions you'll have to answer!

But, this list will give you some idea of the considerations involved in just one goal.

For every goal you set, you will have to think about how reasonable the goal is, how achievable it is and exactly how you plan to accomplish it in the timeframe you have set for yourself.

When it comes to the goals of your family and friends, the emotional attachment and desire to do the right thing may make it hard to think clearly and to accurately plan for how and when these things will happen.

Be honest with yourself and with each other and by all means include your support network in the plan.

Ask your family to come up with ideas about how you can accomplish these things. Brainstorm and leave the door open for crazy ideas.

You'd be surprised at what you might uncover in this way.

Then sit down and pick through the plan and decide which ideas will work and which must be discarded.

As you start to execute your plan, be sure you review it occasionally to ensure that you are still on target and decide if you have to change anything.

Life happens!

And, you may have to change some of your timetables and tasks to incorporate the unexpected changes in your life.

For example, you may plan to take a job that pays less and gives you more time at home to help care for an aging parent.

But, if that parent requires some sort of catastrophic care or expensive medical treatment, you may have to keep the higher paying job to earn the money you need.

If so, are there community support services and low-cost, high-quality caregivers that can come in an work a few hours every day so you can continue to work the longer hours at work to pay for the care?

If not, do you have family members or friends that can pitch in for a little while until you figure out what to do next?

Does the parent have a home that can be sold to help pay for the extra healthcare costs?

Remember, there is always more than one way to solve a problem. Don't panic and don't give up on your work/life balance goals.

Just find another way to accomplish them and be realistic about whether you can achieve them in the same time period.

Perhaps you need to extend your timetable a bit to accommodate the new developments in your life.

That doesn't mean you won't get there.

Just knowing you have a contingency plan will keep you afloat and moving forward.

Remember! PLAN is not just another four-letter word!

Communication is Key

"Life is the continuous adjustment of internal relations to external relations" ~ Herbert Spencer ~

We talked a bit about communication when we discussed family issues, but here the topic is broader.

In general, communication will help you balance life and work by establishing clear boundaries and expectations with others.

This list includes your manager, your friends, your family and your co-workers.

First and foremost, don't assume that others know what is going on. Even if your secretary has a copy of your calendar on her computer, she may not have looked at it today.

Spend a few minutes with your assistants, staff or others in the morning to be sure everyone is on the same page.

Make sure everyone knows your schedule for the day, when you will in the office and available and when you might be away at meetings.

If you are leaving for a business trip, be sure you leave critical contact information so you don't have to fix problems after you return to the office.

If you are an employee and you are expected to perform a certain task, ask questions to be sure you know what has to be done, if there are preferred methods to accomplish the task and when these tasks need to be completed.

Don't leave things to chance.

If you do, your boss may grab you on your way out at the end of your shift and tell you that you have to stay and finish something.

Communicate!

Exchange information with others and find out how they do things. You may learn a better or faster way to get things done and you can get out the door with fewer hours under your belt.

At home, be sure that everyone knows the schedule, when they need to be home for family events and what is expected of them.

If everyone pitches in and understands their role, no one person will be stuck working at chores or doing homework, instead of having some fun family time together.

With friends, be clear about when you are free and be sure your friends understand that they have a place in your life and are important to you.

Make dates and let them know if these dates are subject to change because of late work hours.

Try to plan events when you don't have anything really pressing at work, so you won't be distracted.

You'll find that you get more enjoyment out of your time with friends.

If you have elder care issues, make sure you communicate often with your family and get any doctor's appointment or engagement on your calendar if you are expected to transport or help your parent or ailing uncle.

Be sure that everyone understands what is important to you – your values, priorities and the things you are willing to put aside because of more critical issues.

This will help your staff, family and friends to accommodate and change appointments if they see a conflict.

And never forget that communication is a two-way street. Be sure YOU understand the priorities of your boss, your friends, your co-workers, your wife, your mother and your children.

If you understand how others think and feel you can offer to pitch in and help as needed and this is a favor they will gladly repay the next time YOU need help.

Keep lists and information handy to offer if you have to leave work or home quickly and others need to know what has to be done.

Keep copies of your schedule and itineraries handy when you travel, and always let others know where to reach you and when you will be back.

In meetings, use flip charts to capture thoughts and record agreements and team contracts so you don't waste time trying to figure out what the team decided later on.

If you are in an office job that requires reporting, communicate through email and written reports to be sure everyone knows the schedule, the action items and who is responsible for what tasks.

This will save you time and trouble later.

Whether you are in a meeting at work, talking to a co-worker in a retail store or discussing the family vacation with a family member, practice 'active listening'. Don't tune out!

Communication isn't just talking.

Most of what you'll learn and use to get things done comes from listening to what others are telling you.

Test for understanding to be sure you actually heard what you thought you heard and interpreted it correctly.

If you possess these skills, you have a significant advantage in personal relationships. No matter how little time your family has together each day, if you are really talking to each other and listening to each other, you are a world ahead of your neighbors in maintaining balance in your life and in your relationships.

Think about it for just a moment!

Balance is achieved with the focus and attention you place on a particular thing or person. If a person feels valued and important, if they feel they have your full attention when you are with them, you are well on your way!

Tipping the Scales

"There is time for work. And time for love. That leaves no other time" ~ Coco Chanel ~

If you can't afford to make major changes in your career or your life to get the balance you need and want, there are some other ways to decompress and capitalize on the time you DO have for yourself and your family.

If you institute some simple changes, you will FEEL like you have more time for yourself and the time you have will be more rewarding.

In a moment, we will talk about the affects of stress on your body, your mind and your life and family.

So, hold that thought!

First, we should talk about making the available time 'better'. Many people that have studied and mastered work/life balance are busier than ever!

But they know how to transition between work and social life so that they don't waste time in limbo, trying to shake off the worries of the day and, in the process, ignoring the time they DO have with family members and friends.

Basically, it's all in the approach!

Don't let life run over you!

Get control. Know what you have to do and get it done. Then, when it is time to transition from home to work or from work to home, you will be ready for the transition. To accomplish this, you'll want to think of your 'work time' and your 'personal time' as existing in two different worlds.

Each of these 'worlds' requires different skills and a different focus, but they are both important.

You can use some of the ideas here to create a 'transition' ritual for yourself – one that gets you out of one world and ready for another.

To go from home to work, you can try these things:

Get things ready the night before. Don't wait until the chaos of the morning to pack lunches and iron clothes.

Sign homework and pack your briefcase or car for work the night before, so you don't forget anything.

The less rattled you are going into the day, the less unbalanced you will feel throughout the day.

Set your alarm and get up on time so you don't have to rush. Always allow enough time for that last minute emergency, if you have kids. They have a way of foiling the best-laid plans.

You can try getting up before everyone else does if you think this might work for you.

That will give you a little quiet time to get things done in peace before the rest of the house starts to stir and you are less likely to forget things in the rush.

Some people use this extra quiet time to have a cup of coffee and write out their list for the day. Whatever works for you is fine!

Be sure you don't run short on time to get to work. If you have young children, you have to be creative here. A 'goodbye' routine is a good idea.

One that is fun and easy for the kids to get into will make the drop-off at daycare a lot easier and you will be out the door in no time.

These routines take a few tries to get right, so be patient with yourself and your children.

Perhaps you can make a game of the tasks to be performed on the way out the door by using the familiar 'Simon Says'. "Simon says get your lunch out of the refrigerator".

Others use an imagination game to make the morning go smoothly. When you get to the drop-off point, ask your child to tell you what they will do today and make it fun and outrageous. "What are you going to do today, while I am at work?" "I'm going to climb the castle wall and rescue the beautiful princess. But first I have to kill the dragon that guards her".

As soon as they understand the game, your kids will take it from there!

Focus on what fun things they might do that day, things they will learn and how anxious you will be to hear about what they did when you see them in the evening. And avoid the wrenching goodbyes and feelings of loss.

Have a plan for what you will do if your child is sick or if you wake up to a foot of snow and you can't miss work.

Use your trip to work – by train, car or bus – to read a book you enjoy, make a list of action items for the day, have a cup of your favorite coffee or listen to your favorite CD or meditation tape.

You'll need that sense of Zen and organization to get ready for the day, and you'll greet the problems of the day with calm, and focused approach.

"The harder you work, the harder it is to surrender" ~ *Vince Lombardi* ~

At the end of the day, don't forget to transition back to your 'social' world. Switch out of the work mindset and use your time in the car, train or bus to reprogram yourself.

Consciously leave behind the work worries, make a short list of items to remember for the next day if you need to do so – and then let it go.

Listen to your CDs or read your book and focus on your family and friends. Think about what you will do when you get home and about the things you will share with your family and what they might want to tell you.

Some people close the office door and meditate for a few minutes before they leave or they use the very act of closing the door to 'close the door on the day' as they say.

Whatever works for you is fine!

One woman completes the transition by fixing her make-up, changing her shoes and spraying a fresh scent of perfume in the bathroom on the way out of the office. Now, she's ready for the evening!

An advertising executive changes his clothes to casual clothing and puts on a clown nose for the drive home to get him in a silly mood. He gets a lot of stares by passing drivers, but he loves it.

You may have noticed that firefighters, and police officers never leave the station house in their uniform at the end of their shift.

There are many reasons for that transition but the psychological transition of taking off the 'work clothes' and putting on the street clothes is, nonetheless, a psychological transition that works for nurses, doctors, and firefighters alike.

For anyone that wears a uniform, a suit or other clothing that they don't wear at home, the transition is something they don't have to explain.

The mother that wears a business suit and high heels, is a different person to her children when she changes back into her jeans and t-shirt at home.

Make much of the homecoming, too!

Give hugs and kisses to all and announce your arrival. This will help you to transition and it will give your family the boost they need in seeing you at the end of the day.

And, don't discount laughter as a means of transition from work to home. If you like to listen to stand-up comedians, or talk to a funny friend on the train on the way home, do so. Laughter has a very positive affect on your brain and on your outlook on life.

But, remember that coming home is not always a bed of roses.

Your spouse, children or parents may have had a hard day and they will save their troubles to tell you, their trusted confidante. After a long and hard day at work, the last thing you may feel like doing is to listen to troubles.

It helps to take a breather.

Go change, take a shower and relax for a few moments before you tackle the discussion about bills and health problems.

You can anticipate these discussions by calling home before you leave work to check in. Take the pulse of how things are going at home and find out who is having a bad day.

If you have to pick up your kids on the way home, and you are trapped in the car with a bundle of upset nervous energy, let them blow off steam and tell you their trials of the day for a few minutes.

Then turn on some music they like, settle in and agree that when you get home, everyone will take a deep breath and relax.

Reinforce that HOME is a soothing place! A place they can go to be with those that care about them and to get away from the problems of the day.

If YOU have a really tough day, tell your family that and ask for a few minutes to compose yourself before you join in the fray.

Be sure that they know that they have done nothing wrong and that you are just taking the time for yourself because of the day you had at work.

As you practice some of these techniques, you are bound to come up with your own ideas and rituals and you should try them and make liberal use of those that work for you, in order to help yourself with this transition.

Dealing with Stress

Perhaps the most pervasive and difficult problem to solve in life balancing is that of stress. Whether you are at work or at home, there is likely some stress in your life, and that stress can interfere with your enjoyment of your career and your social life.

Stress is what we experience when we must adjust to the constant and conflicting demands of our lives. If you like your job and work long hours, if you are very competitive and always trying to win, you may experience a more positive form of stress.

But for most of us, when we experience unremitting stress, and we don't know how to handle it, it makes us angry, frustrated, irritable, depressed and fatigued. We may get headaches or develop an ulcer, or perhaps we suffer from insomnia. Unless we can learn to eliminate or mitigate stress, we will function poorly on the job, at home and with friends.

Recognize that stress is real and that it can affect your health, your happiness and your relationships. There are lots of ways to defeat stress, and you'll need to find the right one for yourself.

Here are some links that will get you started:

http://www.mindtools.com/smpage.html

http://www.psychwww.com/mtsite/smpage.html

http://www.hyperstress.com/

http://www.extension.umn.edu/distribution/familydevelopment/DE7269.html

There are any number of other sites that focus on stress, many of them sponsored by universities and containing some great information and ideas about specific types of stress and stressful events.

Depending on where most of your stress is, you may want to focus in a different area. If your boss is a major stressor in your life, if there is abuse or a hostile environment at work, you have a different problem than the stress that comes from caring for an ailing parent, spouse or child or the stress that comes from financial troubles.

But, regardless of the cause of your stress, the effects are the same. Extreme stress can be short-lived, as in stress after the death of a loved one, or it can be long-term.

You may ask how and why stress figures into your work/life balance goals.

It is very simple. Whether you are trying to balance your time or simply improve the quality of your life, it is important to acknowledge stress and to understand that there IS something called positive stress, and something called negative stress.

Positive stress is the stress you feel when you are planning your daughter's wedding or when you are about to make an important presentation.

You may be happy about the event and looking forward to the occasion, but that doesn't mean there is no stress.

That kind of stress is not harmful and can be quite invigorating. But, negative stress IS harmful, especially if it occurs over a long period of time.

Consider on-the-job stress, or stress in a relationship because of poor communication or the absence of focused time spent with a loved one – all of these things can damage your health and the quality of your life.

So, start by identifying the stressors in your life, and looking for the places you feel most stressed.

Then address the source of the stress, if you can. Because, the best way to approach stress is head-on. Later, we'll talk about how you can relieve and mitigate stress if you are in a situation where you cannot eliminate it altogether.

But first, let's look at how and when you can take charge and what you can change.

As we said earlier, you have to start by ***identifying the stressor(s) and taking stock of your reactions to this stress.***
Notice the emotional and physical responses you have to stress. Do your muscles tense? Do you get headaches? Do you get nauseous or have stomach pain? Do you get nervous and irritable? Don't pretend it isn't an issue. Be objective about your reactions.
Next, figure out what you can change and how you can relieve or eliminate the stress. Can you take those tasks or situations that cause you the most stress and schedule or spread them out so that you can tackle them when you are prepared and rested, rather than taking them on in a whirlwind with other things going on at the same time?
Can you shorten the time you are exposed to the stress? If your boss is a great stressor in your life, don't schedule a one-hour meeting with her if you can avoid it. Instead, try stopping by her office to talk briefly, or if you must schedule time, schedule it during times of the day when you are less likely to feel harried.
And keep the meetings short and to the point. Stay on track and don't get off on tangents that may make the situation more stressful.

If you have times of day or situations where you are under a lot of stress, try to take a break. Walk outside for a few minutes or go to get coffee. Break the pattern and then come back refreshed to finish the task.

If you focus on making changes to avoid the stress – for example, extending timetables to make a project more feasible, or setting more realistic goals – you will hit the problem at its root cause instead of trying to run and catch up all the time.

Try to analyze and alter your reaction to stress. Much of the damage done by stress is not done by the event itself, but instead by your body's reaction to the event.

Your body and mind perceive danger and react accordingly and everything becomes exaggerated. The danger seems more threatening, the task more daunting, and the outcome more dismal.

Reason with yourself and ask "what is the worse that can happen?" Are you overreacting to the stressor and making your fear and emotional response worse?

Is everything as critical and time-sensitive as you think or are you just overly sensitive to pleasing everyone, all at the same time?

Don't obsess over the negative factors and predict failure. Stick to the positive and, even if there are issues, focus on the things that worked well and note them.

THEN revisit the places that didn't work so well, with a more objective eye toward improving the process, and try not to place or take blame. Just be sure to learn from your experience and the next time it will go better.

And remember, everyone makes mistakes!

Whatever you do, don't go into a project or situation by predicting doom. You will never succeed that way and in the process, you will endure the stress of trying to consider every 'what if' and failure in the book.

Learn how to mitigate stress by diffusing it when it happens. When your heart starts to race and your palms get sweaty, take a two-minute time out and try some deep, slow breathing. It will reduce your heart rate and bring your mind back into focus.

Consciously relax the muscles in your shoulders and neck, the muscles around your jaw and in your scalp. Unclench your hands and close your eyes. Just for a moment.

You'll be glad you took the break and so will your body!

Take care of yourself. Exercise three or four times a week. Cardio-vascular workouts like aerobics, rapid walking or running are great to relieve stress and strengthen your heart and lungs.

Don't eat fast food. Try to eat a well-balanced diet and avoid stress responses like smoking and drinking. Take frequent breaks. Remember you can still think through problems and get things accomplished while you take a quick walk or go for a glass of water.

You don't have to be at your desk to get things done!

Maintain supportive friendships and relationships and don't let them die on the vine. It is this replenishment that will keep you going. Set your own goals and don't let others force you into situations you don't like.

You will always have some stress and frustration, but if you know yourself and if you build your reserves to meet these challenges, you will lead a much more balanced life and work stressors will not creep over into your personal life.

What if you've done all the right things and you still suffer the effects of stress? What if that stress is not something you can easily change?

Remember, we said that you could always change your reaction to the stress.

But, sometimes, just knowing you have to calm down doesn't help much.

We mentioned exercise as a way to mitigate stress, but there are a lot of other structured approaches to mental and physical relaxation, from meditation and yoga to biofeedback, and all of these are beneficial.

Pick the one that works for you.

Here are a few ideas to get you started:

Deep Breathing – Learning to breathe, deep into your abdomen and to slow your body down sounds easy, but it takes a bit of practice.

However, you can do it anywhere. On a bus, train or plane and once you've learned it you will wonder how you ever got along without it.

Because the increased oxygenation of your blood brings more clarity to your brain, you will double the benefit by being able to solve problems better, as well!

Biofeedback is a method of relaxation that helps you to control your responses to and change how your body and mind react. Your brain 'learns' how to adjust as you use monitoring equipment to track your heart rate, muscle tension, blood pressure, and skin temperature.

Guided Imagery uses affirmations and relaxing images to calm and focus your mind and body, and control your breathing so you are more relaxed.

It is easy to learn and the more you practice the better and faster your brain will response to the cues, putting you into a state of relaxation more quickly every time.

Meditation has become one of the most popular techniques to achieve relaxation. It is not tied to any religious belief, and can be learned alone through self-study or in groups. Meditation changes your brain waves, and alters the response to stress in your mind, your emotions, and your body.

You can start and end your day with a brief meditation, and eventually, you may find it so helpful that you will employ this technique wherever you are, and whenever you feel stress.

Focused Muscle Relaxation teaches the student to tighten and relax groups of muscles in turn until the entire body is in a state of relaxation. It is easy to learn and can be mastered quickly and effectively with good results.

Yoga is an ancient form of exercise that is based on the connection between the muscles and organs in the body, breathing techniques and the combined effects on the mind. The goal of yogic practice is to restore balance to the body and your emotions through postures, stretching and breathing exercises.

Other forms of exercise, like cardio-vascular workouts, running and walking will increase the release of certain 'good' chemicals in your brain, thereby relieving stress, frustration and anger and helping you to sleep.

If you suffer from stress-related insomnia, you should consider trying one or more of the solutions we've outlined here. It will help you get the sleep you need to function well, and to keep you healthy and balanced.

Keeping it Fresh and Flexible

As with any plan, your plan for work/life balance must be kept fresh and flexible. Be sure you allow for contingencies and guard against backsliding.

Old habits die-hard and you may find yourself in need of a refresher to stay on track.

Look at your plan often and keep talking about it with your friends and family and co-workers. The more you reinforce its important to yourself and others, the less chance you will fall back into your old ways.

Remember that nothing ever goes just as planned, so be ready for the unexpected and don't let it get you down.

If your plan did not include a contingency for a particular event, just sit down and look over the plan again and make room for some new ideas to address the problem you face.

Don't be discouraged if you hit a snag.

"For a long time it had seemed to me that life was about to begin - real life. But there was always some obstacle in the way. Something to be got through first, some unfinished business, time still to be served, a debt to be paid. Then life would begin. At last it dawned on me that these obstacles were my life"

~ Fr. Alfred D'Souza ~

Remember that it will take awhile for the world to catch up to you and while many companies and people may not understand the need for balance, the fact that you do, may save your life and your relationships.

If those around you fail to recognize the importance of your efforts and scoff at your taking a lower paying job or choosing to stay home with a sick child, remain secure in the knowledge that you are running a marathon, not a sprint and that in the end, you will finish the race well!

You may be breaking new ground. You may be a role model. And, that position is not always easy. Pioneers have hard work to do, but they ARE the first to see the beauty of the new horizon.

So, stick to your plan! You will get better at this as your old habits die. Remember to exercise self-discipline and have the courage of your convictions.

Remember to pay attention to the important things and keep things in perspective.

Don't spin your wheels or expend too much energy on the things you can't change or the things you don't feel are important.

Just because someone else tells you it is important, doesn't mean you have to believe them.

Keep the plan and the perspective fresh and if one thing doesn't work, try another. It is your commitment to the change that is important.

And if you find another way to get there, that is just fine!

It may not turn out exactly as you expected, but your focus on the goal of balance is the important thing! Without that focus, you can't change anything!

Don't be afraid to get advice from others you trust if you get stuck on the path. You don't have to do this alone.

Summary

"Be glad of life because it gives you the chance to love and to work and to play and to look up at the stars" ~ Henry Van Dyke ~

We've covered a lot of ground in a very short period of time, and you may want to review this information again to make sure you've got it all.

The concepts are simple, and although you may find yourself wondering if all of them relate to work/life balance, you will find answers as you implement the steps we've outlined here.

Each of these steps is designed to address a different part of the problem.

Having enough time and focus to appreciate your life outside of work is one thing.

Having the mental, emotional and physical stamina to do it all is another.

Understanding how to keep your life in balance, and what the factors involved in a long-term commitment, is also important.

If you can't manage your time, you will never have enough of it, no matter how few hours you work in a week.

Taking a step back to look at how you got to where you are and what issues you'll need to resolve to backtrack – that's important too.

Think of this as a primer, of sorts. Of course, the particulars are yours to figure out and your specific issues are different than the issues your neighbor will face, but there are many common factors.

As we said at the beginning of this discussion, you'll need a plan. So, let's review some of the key components.

You can adjust and tweak your plan along the way, as you need to make changes, but getting the plan in place is the first and most critical step.

- Sit down with a pencil and paper and gather your thoughts and expectations.
- Talk to your family, your boss, your co-workers and your friends and get their thoughts.
- Then set your goals!
- Make the plan and move forward.

🕑 Adjust the plan along the way if you need to do so and be realistic about what you can accomplish and how long it will take.

🕑 Keep the lines of communication open and keep people informed about your goals and your progress and about what is important to you.

🕑 Learn to manage your time better so you can leverage the free time you have to use it as you wish.

🕑 Schedule and keep commitments with your family and friends.

🕑 Find ways to improve your productivity and learn to transition from work to home and back again so that you are truly 'present' in every situation and not spinning your wheels thinking about other things.

🕑 Don't get distracted!

🕑 Exercise self-discipline and stay committed. Pay attention and listen to others and do it right the first time so you don't have to do it over again!

🕑 Learn to handle and diffuse stress and eliminate it from your life wherever you can.

🕑 Be optimistic and positive.

🕑 Understand that work/life balance is key to your health and happiness and it can actually make you more productive at work and give you a better quality of time with your family and friends.

And, so we come to the end of our journey!

Now, it's your turn to get the plan on paper.

You can do this!

Take control of your life and live it to the fullest.

Keep your priorities straight!

Remember! You don't live to work – you work to live!

"I don't want to get to the end of my life and find that I lived just the length of it. I want to have lived the width of it as well" ~ Diane Ackerman ~